CONTENTS

ABUNDANT LIFE THROUGH JESUS CHRIST, THE BONDAGE BREAKER

I came that they may have life,
and have it abundantly.

JOHN 10:10

Those words were spoken by Jesus Christ, the Good Shepherd. He gave His life for us, His sheep, so that we might experience life abundantly and life eternal. But for too many believers, the words of that promise sound empty, and the reality seems far away.

Does Jesus's promise sound empty to you? Do you feel far away from the joy and peace that other Christians seem to experience? Instead of enjoying a productive life of freedom in Jesus Christ, do you seem to be in bondage to fear, anger, or depression? Are you struggling with habits you can't break, thoughts or inner voices you can't silence, or sinful behaviors you can't escape?

It's for people like you that I've written *The Bondage Breaker* and this study guide. *The Bondage Breaker* explains your position of life, freedom, protection, and authority in Christ. It warns of your vulnerability to very real demonic influences that are intent on robbing you of your freedom, and tells you of your need to submit to God and resist the devil. The book also presents The Steps to Freedom in Christ, which will help you walk free of the enemy's designs on your life.

But simply reading about these things is quite different from living out the freedom that Jesus desires you to have, and that's why I've written this guide—to help you apply to your own life what you read about in *The Bondage Breaker*. I encourage you to work through this book slowly and thoroughly, and to pray each step of the way.

As you work through these lessons, you'll be studying more closely the scriptures I refer to in the text; taking a closer look at your own life, past and present; and, I pray, opening yourself to the work of God in your life. Linger over the passages of Scripture. Let God speak to your heart and use His Word to work in your life. May this be an opportunity for you to draw closer to your loving and powerful heavenly Father.

It is also my prayer that you will be able to personalize the Bible's powerful words of truth, believe its life-changing message of hope, and experience the freedom and abundant life that are available to you through the work of Jesus Christ, your Shepherd and your Bondage Breaker.

—Neil Anderson

PART ONE

TAKE COURAGE!

1

YOU DON'T HAVE TO LIVE IN THE SHADOWS

ARE YOU LIVING IN THE SHADOWS?

Dear God,

Where are You? How can You watch and not help me? I hurt so bad, and You don't even care...I love You, but You seem so far away. I can't hear You or feel You or see You, but I'm supposed to believe You're here...

Perhaps you can identify with this woman's feelings. Perhaps you've felt this way in the past or are feeling this way now. The message of this chapter—and this book—is that you don't have to live in the shadows.

Why are you reading *The Bondage Breaker* and working through this study guide? What do you hope to learn about God's ability to work in your life and His power over Satan?

Read again the following passage from page 26:

Over the past 40 years, I have encountered hundreds

of Christians like the one who wrote this heartrending note. Most of them didn't attempt suicide, but many of them talked about dark impressions to do so. Nearly all of them admitted to the presence of "them"—inner urges or voices which badgered them, tempted and taunted them, accused them, or threatened them. We often tell people who come to our ministry for help that they will struggle with thoughts such as, *Don't go; they can't help you*—or they will think disruptive thoughts in first-person singular, like *I don't want to go*, or *I've tried this before, and it didn't work...*

Others may not be hearing voices, but their minds are so distracted that their daily walk with Christ is unfulfilling and unproductive. When they try to pray, they are tempted and bombarded by all sorts of things around them. When they attempt to read the Bible, they can't concentrate, and when they finish a chapter, they can't remember any of what they read...Instead of being victorious, productive, joy-filled Christians, they trudge through life under a cloud, trying to hang on until the rapture.

Where, if at all, do you see yourself in this description? Where might the enemy be deceiving you or robbing you of the joy of the Christian life?

Define "bondage" in your own words.

What do you feel when you hear that word?

COMMON MISCONCEPTIONS ABOUT SPIRITUAL BONDAGE

There is much confusion about the presence and activity of demons in the world today. This confusion keeps many Christians in bondage to a power they don't acknowledge. After reading pages 27-34, write out in your own words arguments against the following misconceptions about the spiritual world.

1. Demons were active when Christ was on earth, but their activity has subsided.

2. What the early church called demonic activity we now understand to be mental illness.

3. Some problems are only psychological, and some are only spiritual.

4. Christians cannot be affected by demons.

5. Demonic influence is evident only in extreme or violent behavior and gross sin.

6. Freedom from spiritual bondage is the result of a power encounter with demonic forces.

Which misconceptions have you accepted as truth? Rebut those ideas with passages from Scripture that refer to God's power, His truth, or Satan's defeat. Write out those verses here and on an index card to carry with you to remind you of your victory over Satan through Christ.

KNOW THE ENEMY AND THE VICTOR

Look up the following passages. Write down the phrases used to describe Satan.

—John 8:44

—John 10:10

—1 John 5:19

—Revelation 12:9

Compare those terms for Satan with the following descriptions of Jesus and His Holy Spirit.

—John 6:48

—John 14:6

—John 16:13

—Isaiah 9:6

THE ARMOR OF GOD

Read Ephesians 6:12 and 2 Corinthians 10:3-5. Note the present-tense verbs. What did Paul say believers will encounter in this world?

Believers are not left defenseless in the face of the enemy. Read Ephesians 6:10-18.

—List the six components of the "full armor of God." (We'll look at them more closely in chapter 6.)

—When should we be praying?

—What does the role of prayer suggest about the nature of spiritual warfare?

SETTING CAPTIVES FREE

Why is there so little instruction on "setting captives free" in the epistles (see page 35 in *The Bondage Breaker*)? Look again at the section in which I point to the cross, and give two reasons. Read the scriptural support, then explain the reasons in your own words.

—Matthew 28:18 and Colossians 2:15

—Ephesians 1:18-21 and 2:5-6

When one woman was experiencing deep spiritual, mental, and emotional turmoil, she wrote a letter to God, which I quoted at the beginning of the chapter. Take time now to write your own letter to God. Cry to Him for help. Share what's on your heart. Ask Him to work in your life.

—If you can—and you may not be able to now—write a letter from God in response to your letter to Him. In it, personalize verses from the Bible. Let God address you specifically through His Word by weaving your name into the texts you choose.

—Maybe at this point in your journey, the darkness is too thick for you to imagine God saying anything to you. If so, read the letter to the Lost Sheep on pages 36-37, and replace "Lost Sheep" with your name.

THE TRUTH SHALL SET YOU FREE

The truth of God's love and His power is what liberates Christians from the hold of the enemy. Which of the following verses, or which verse of your own choosing, is an especially effective reminder of that fact? Write it out here. (You might also want to write it on an index card to carry with you or to put in a strategic place where it can remind you of God's power over evil, confusion, and despair.)

—John 14:6

—John 17:15,17

—Philippians 4:8

—Romans 8:38-39

—1 Peter 3:21-22

After reading this chapter, what new truth have you realized, or what truth are you now seeing more clearly?

Spend a few minutes with the Lord. Share your letter with Him, and listen for His quiet response. Share your fears and doubts with your heavenly Father, your almighty King. The prayer "I do believe; help my unbelief" (Mark 9:24) has proven effective for many saints through the centuries.

2

FINDING YOUR WAY IN THE WORLD

THE DEVIL AT WORK

What are some ways the deceiver is at work in the world today?

On page 40 of *The Bondage Breaker* I share that

> postmodernism has undermined objective truth, and civil discourse about subjects that really matter is nearly impossible in a public forum. Authoritative structures are crumbling, and educational administrators are capitulating to the demands of a spoiled generation. The trend is to be spiritual but not religious, yet no attempt is made to define what it means to be spiritual. Postmodernists argue that what is spiritual for me may not be for you, and what is true for you may not be true for me!

What are some of the results that can be expected when truth and authority are defied?

Why do you think the deceiver likes it when people question truth? Do you agree that only God's truth can be trusted? Why or why not?

THE TWO-TIER WORLDVIEW

What is the basic difference between the Western worldview and the Eastern worldview?

What is the biblical reality about the relationship between the natural and the spiritual or supernatural?

What do the following passages suggest about the supernatural?

　　—Ephesians 6:10-12

　　—Romans 8:38-39

　　—1 Peter 3:22

　　—Colossians 1:16

　　—1 Corinthians 10:20-21

Why must we who are Christians include the kingdom of darkness in our worldview?

A young woman had developed physical symptoms that were diagnosed as multiple sclerosis. After she renounced her request for a thorn in the flesh and prayed to be freed from any influence by Satan in her life, the symptoms disappeared. Most doctors and psychologists would not even consider her condition to be a spiritual problem.

—Why do many believers today, along with doctors and psychologists, tend not to consider the possibility of spiritual causes for physical ailments?

—What is the result of not considering the possible spiritual basis for physical problems?

LIVING IN THE EXCLUDED MIDDLE

Scripture teaches that supernatural, spiritual forces are at work in the world. What do the following passages teach or illustrate about those forces?

—Mark 5:1-20

—Luke 4:33-37

—Luke 13:11-12

—1 John 3:8

—Hebrews 2:14

"When people have symptoms, we have been conditioned in our Western way of thinking to look for a natural or physical explanation first, and if that doesn't work, we say, 'There is nothing left to do but pray'" (page 45).

—Do you agree with that statement? Why or why not?

—Can you think of ways that spiritual problems in our lives can affect how we think and act?

GETTING SPIRITUAL WITHOUT GOD

"The center of [*the secular*] worldview is self: What will *I* get out of this? What about *my* needs? I'm doing *my* thing with my iPhone and iPad. The problem with pride is that it has I as its center" (page 46).

—Why is self such a powerful tool for Satan to use?

—Why are selfish ambition and pride effective weapons for Satan to use against the kingdom of God?

Look at Matthew 16:13-16,21-23.

—What does Peter confidently proclaim in verses 13-16?

—What news does he react to in verse 22?

—Why is this reaction satanic in principle? In other words, what motivated Peter to say what he did?

THE VIEW FROM THE CROSS

How is a situation where people "are their own gods" a logical extension of self-interest?

Why is being one's own god so appealing?

And why is being one's own god so wrong?

Where does being one's own god lead?

Turn to Genesis chapters 2 and 3, the account of Adam and Eve in the Garden of Eden.

—What did God command in Genesis 2:15-17?

—How did the serpent (and Eve herself!) twist those words in Genesis 3:1-5?

Why don't humans succeed at being their own gods?

Look at what Jesus taught His disciples in Matthew 16:24-27. Why is obedience to this teaching crucial to having a healthy spiritual life?

Jesus's words in Matthew 16:24-27 offer six guidelines for freedom from bondage to the world system and the devil who inspires that bondage.

Deny Yourself

How is denying yourself different from self-denial?

What do you do when you deny yourself?

Why is denying oneself essential to spiritual freedom?

Pick Up Your Cross Daily

What has the cross of Christ provided for believers?

What do the following scriptures teach about who we are because of Jesus's death on the cross?

—1 Peter 1:18-19

—1 John 3:1-3

—Colossians 3:4

What does the phrase "pick up your cross" mean to you?

How does the command to pick up your cross counter Satan's invitation to be your own god?

Follow Christ

Where will Christ lead you if you follow Him?

What benefits come from following Christ? Let the following scriptures serve as a starting point for your list.

—John 10:27-28

—Romans 8:14

—Romans 12:2

Can you think of other scriptures to add?

—

—

Sacrifice the Lower Life to Gain the Higher Life

Jesus said, "Everyone who has left houses or brothers or sisters or father or mother or children or farms for My name's sake, will receive many times as much, and will inherit eternal life" (Matthew 19:29). What does this statement teach about that which is truly valuable?

How can pursuing the things of the world keep you from attaining spiritual things?

What is worth pursuing, according to 1 Timothy 4:8?

Sacrifice the Pleasure of Things to Gain the Pleasure of Life

Look around. What lasting pleasures does the world offer?

Now look at Galatians 5:22-23. What blessings or fruits does the Holy Spirit offer?

According to your checkbook, what are you pursuing—the pleasures of the world, or the blessings of the Spirit?

Read Luke 10:38-42.

—What was Martha interested in? And Mary?

—Are you more like Martha or Mary?

—How does this passage encourage you or convict you?

Sacrifice the Temporal to Gain the Eternal

According to Hebrews 11:24-26, how does Moses illustrate the principle of sacrificing the temporal to gain the eternal?

How have you sacrificed the temporal to gain the eternal?

A LOOK AT YOURSELF

In what ways are you living independently of God right now?

—Confess those areas where you have been doing things your own way, and relinquish control to Christ.

—Ask God to show you those areas in which you are lord, yet don't see it.

—Ask God to forgive you for usurping His rightful place as Lord of every area of your life.

—Renew your commitment to living with Jesus as Lord of your life.

3

YOU HAVE EVERY RIGHT TO BE FREE

HOW DO YOU PERCEIVE YOURSELF?

Just as I asked Lydia, I want to ask you how you perceive yourself. Be as specific as possible (are you good? evil? somewhere in between?), and then consider how well your perceptions line up with the truth of Scripture.

Look at the list of scriptures that tell us who we are "in Christ" on pages 54-56.

—Read aloud these biblical statements of affirmation.

—Choose one or two passages to memorize as a reminder of who you are in Christ.

Why would Satan want to convince you that you are worthless and evil?

The following concepts are foundational to your freedom from spiritual conflict as a child of God. They are also foundational to freedom from

Satan's efforts to convince you that you are worthless and evil. Look up the supporting scriptures and summarize what they say about the concepts listed below. And remember that when we read a truth, we are to believe it. Believe these words of truth as you meditate on them!

YOU ARE A CHILD OF GOD

—1 John 3:1-3 (What is our relationship to God the Father, based on what He has done? What is our hope now?)

—John 1:12 (What has God given to us?)

—Romans 8:16-17 (Who is it that affirms our place before God?)

Think again about being a child of God. How will believing this about yourself affect your life?

Mention two or three reasons why understanding and affirming who we are in Christ is so important.

YOU ARE SPIRITUALLY AND THEREFORE ETERNALLY ALIVE

—Read Ephesians 1:1-13, especially verses 7 and 13. What is our standing in relation to Christ once we accept Him as Savior and Lord?

—According to 1 Corinthians 6:19-20, who lives in you?

—What promise do you find in Romans 8:9-11?

How can you dispute Satan's accusation that you are not spiritually and therefore eternally alive?

Read 1 John 4:11-12. When have you "seen God" in the love of His people? Be specific.

YOU ARE A NEW CREATION IN CHRIST

—Read Romans 5:8-11. Why can you rejoice?

—How were you saved from your sins, according to Ephesians 2:1-5?

—Based on Colossians 1:13-14,22, describe the new creation you are in Christ.

How can Satan use the thought that we are only "sinners saved by grace" to bind us?

What word does Scripture use to describe your actual status? (See Colossians 1:12.) What reassurance does that word give you?

Look again at the list of Scripture verses on pages 54-56, and list out for yourself some of the things we have gained through being identified with Christ.

How are your thoughts, words, and actions different since you became a believer? How does your behavior reflect the truth that you are a new creature in Christ (2 Corinthians 5:17)?

You Can Be Victorious over Sin and Death

Let the material on pages 59-62 help you grasp the meaning of Romans 6, then summarize its major points by answering the questions below.

—According to Romans 6:1-11, what relationship with sin did God allow Jesus to have? Why?

—Read Romans 6:12-13. How are believers to relate to sin now?

—What choice does every believer have, according to Romans 12:1?

What—and whose—experience is necessary for you to be dead to sin? (See pages 61-62.) Praise God for that truth!

Why is Romans 12:1 important to someone who wants to be victorious over sin and the flesh? What does the verse say about a person's role in the victory?

You Can Be Free from the Power of Sin

Read carefully my conversation with Dan on pages 63-67.

—How many players are there? (See Romans 7:15-17.) Identify them.

—Which player is bad? (See Romans 7:18-21.) Why is that good news for Dan and you?

—According to Romans 7:22-25, where does the battle rage? What is inflicting the pain? Who is the source of victory?

Where do you most identify with Dan (and the apostle Paul)?

What words from my conversation with Dan offer you new insight and hope?

A LOOK BACK...

Which of the five foundational truths discussed in this chapter speaks most directly to your present situation?

What comfort, encouragement, and correction did the discussion of these truths offer you?

AND A LOOK AT YOURSELF

How could your actions more clearly reflect your belief that you are a dearly loved and accepted child of God? What can you do to better live like a child of God? Be specific.

What passages of Scripture in this chapter did you find particularly helpful to you with regard to areas in which you are in bondage? Choose one passage to commit to memory, and begin memorizing it today.

4

YOU CAN WIN THE
BATTLE FOR YOUR MIND

THINK ABOUT YOUR OWN BATTLE

I n chapter 3, Dan and I had a conversation about the struggle in his mind over his feelings about who he was. As we read through Romans 7, he began to see himself in a new light.

He was asking the same question that so many believers have: "If the scriptures about who I am in Christ are true, then how come I still struggle with the same thoughts and feelings I had before I became a Christian?"

Have you wrestled with this question yourself? Think about it for a moment before you go on.

—What was Paul's exhortation to believers with regard to their minds (Romans 12:2)?

—Why is this so important?

—In Romans 12:2, who is doing the transforming?

—How does this help us with any incorrect thoughts or wrong feelings we might have?

MENTAL STRONGHOLDS

How are defense mechanisms similar to "strongholds" ("fortresses" in 2 Corinthians 10:3-5)?

—What is the answer to our problem with strongholds?

—How can we "unlearn" strongholds?

SATAN'S SCHEMES

What is Satan's aim in the battle for our minds?

Paul expressed his concern for the Corinthians in 2 Corinthians 10:5; 2:10-11; and 11:3 (pages 71-72). How can Satan's schemes damage our relationships with others, especially other believers?

"After helping thousands [of people] find their freedom in Christ, I can testify that unforgiveness is the major reason people remain in bondage to the past" (page 72). The Steps, which appear in the Appendix, deal with forgiveness more extensively, but try to list right now two or three areas in which the Holy Spirit may be prompting you to exercise forgiveness toward other people.

SATAN AND OUR MINDS

With your Bible open to Genesis 3:1-13 (the account of the fall of Adam and Eve), consider Satan's strategies in the lives of David, Judas, and Ananias and Sapphira. How do these strategies relate to the original lie?

—What does this also tell you about the type of thoughts Satan will try to put in your mind?

—Does it help you to know that many other believers have experienced Satan's deceptions in their thoughts? Why?

"NOT AGAINST FLESH AND BLOOD"

In your copy of the book *The Bondage Breaker*, go back and reread the first part of chapter 1, "You Don't Have to Live in the Shadows" (pages 25-27). Do you view this woman's experience differently after reading "Not Against Flesh and Blood" (pages 74-76)? Why or why not?

What would you say to her about her inner conflict?

The struggle of the believer is "not against flesh and blood." What are some of the ways we may try to "explain this away"?

BRAIN VERSUS MIND

In what way is the illustration about computer hardware and software helpful for understanding demonic spiritual influence?

It's important to be able to distinguish between normal dreams and demonically influenced dreams. How can we make this determination?

Read Psalm 119:147-148. What strategy does this passage suggest for combatting deceptive and discouraging thoughts that come at night?

THE BATTLE IS REAL

When a person says, "It's all in your mind," it's like saying, "That doesn't really exist." What have you learned that might make you respond differently when someone tells you they're hearing thoughts in their mind?

In a scenario involving a frightened child, what can a parent say to reassure the child?

How would you apply this to your own life?

Look again at the experiences of various people whom I describe (pages 79-82). What is crucial for helping people to enjoy quietness and freedom in Christ?

TAKING EVERY THOUGHT CAPTIVE

Why, in one sense, does it not make any difference to us where lying or condemning thoughts come from?

What promise does God give us with regard to our prayers? (See Philippians 4:7.)

Why does being bitter and unforgiving cause so much damage? (See James 4:6.)

FREEDOM IS AVAILABLE

Which defense mechanisms (see page 70) do you think are present in your own life?

How do you now see that God can give (or is giving) you victory in these areas?

List some Scripture verses from this chapter that can help you be victorious in the battle for your mind. Write two or three of these verses on a card to carry with you so they can remind you that victory is available.

Turn to Philippians 4:4-9. Write out the commands to be obeyed and the promises to be claimed. Think about how the commands and promises relate to the battle for your mind. Spend some time asking God to open your eyes to your life and position in Christ that make your understanding and obedience possible. Thank God also for making freedom available to you through His Son.

5

CONFRONTING THE REBEL PRINCE

CARRYING JESUS'S BADGE OF AUTHORITY

Before we discuss in detail the reality and present activity of Satan and his demons, you need to understand your position of authority in Christ as it relates to the spiritual realm.

Your resistance of the devil is based on the authority you possess in Christ.

—The disciples' resistance was based on the authority they possessed in Christ. In Luke 10:17, they acknowledged this authority as they rejoiced over the results of their ministry. What was crucial to their success?

—The disciples were spiritually in tune enough to know that demons existed and were a force to be reckoned with. Why do you think that too few Christians today acknowledge the reality of demons?

Turn to Luke 10:19-20. What was and is to be the main priority of those who want to heal and release people from the bondage of demons?

What part does our position in Christ play in our authority over the kingdom of darkness?

Look at Matthew 4:3-4. On whom did Jesus depend in His resistance of the devil? On whom are we to depend?

The Right and the Ability to Rule

It is *truth* that sets you free, not the knowledge of error. You would have no authority at all if it weren't for your identity as a child of God and your position in Christ. *Who you are* must always take precedence over *what you do*.

Jesus gave His disciples both authority and power over demons.

—What is authority?

—What is power?

—Why did Jesus's disciples need both authority and power?

What lesson does the story of David and Goliath teach you about your ability to resist Satan and his demons? (See 1 Samuel 17 and page 89.)

What is the basis for success in finding our freedom in Christ and helping others to do the same? (It's not education, calling, or personality!)

Pulling Rank

Too often spiritual warfare involving God, Satan, and us is viewed as a tug-of-war on a horizontal plane, but this picture is not right. What is the biblical and therefore correct view? (Matthew 28:18; Romans 13:1; and Luke 10:17 will help you answer this question.)

According to the text, why does the kingdom of darkness exert such negative influence in the world and in the lives of Christians?

As we saw in the preceding chapter, what we believe affects how we act. How do our beliefs about our authority in the spiritual realm affect our actions?

What does 1 John 5:18 promise believers?

How should we respond when the enemy tries to incite fear in us?

THE RICHES OF OUR
INHERITANCE IN CHRIST

Do you and I enjoy the same claim to Christ's authority in the spiritual realm as those who were personally sent out by Him? Yes!

How is our position even more advantageous than that of the early disciples? Compare Mark 3:14-15 (the "then" picture) with Ephesians 1:3-13 (the "now" picture).

Paul prayed that the believers' inner eyes would be opened. What did he want the Christians at Ephesus, and us today, to see?

How can our blindness prevent us from exercising the authority of Christ in our lives?

The Depth and Breadth of Authority

According to Ephesians 1:19-23, what is the power source for the authority we have in Christ?

How does Paul identify the expanse of Christ's authority?

In which realm is this tremendous authority in Christ active through us?

Authority Conferred

The moment you receive Christ, you are seated with Him in the heavenlies. Your identity as a child of God and your authority over spiritual powers are things you have *right now.*

Open your Bible to Ephesians 1 and 2.

> —What was God's supreme act of power and authority? (See 1:19-21.)

> —According to 2:4-6, what did God do for you and me?

The resurrection of Christ from the tomb and our resurrection from spiritual death happened at the same time. Look at Colossians 2:15. What happened to Satan at that moment?

Despite the facts presented in Ephesians and Colossians, many believers fail to experience victory in their lives. By what means is Satan able to introduce defeat into the lives of Christians?

How do you react to these biblical facts about the depth and breadth of the authority available to you in Jesus Christ? What rethinking does this cause you to do about the world situation? About believers who have allowed themselves to be held in bondage and live in defeat?

Qualified for Kingdom Work

I believe there are at least four qualifications for demonstrating authority over rulers and authorities in the spiritual realm.

Belief

—Why is confidence an important component of belief? (See Ephesians 1:19.)

—What belief is fundamental to breaking the bondage of Satan? And why is that belief crucial?

Humility

—How do you define "humility"?

—In whom or what do we place our confidence when we want to exercise our authority over Satan? (See John 15:5.)

—How did Jesus model authority?

Boldness

—How do you define "boldness"? Who serves as an example of boldness for you?

—How can knowledge lead to increased boldness?

—Turn to Revelation 21:6-8. What fate awaits the cowardly?

Dependence

—The authority over Satan that we have in Christ is essential for carrying out our ministry. According to the text, when are we to exercise our authority? And on whom are we to depend when we do so?

—When is the only time we aren't to submit to the authority of government, work, home, and church?

FREE FROM FEAR

When we boldly and humbly exercise the authority that Christ has conferred on us over the spiritual realm, we experience the freedom we all have in Christ.

—Think back on your own life. When have you experienced freedom from fear, and how do you relate this to your exercise of your authority in Christ?

—Look at John 8:31-32. How does this add to your understanding of your freedom in Christ?

What step can you take today to clarify your perspective on the power
of Jesus Christ over Satan? Perhaps it will mean reviewing this chapter,
looking at the Gospel accounts of how Jesus operated against the powers of darkness, or fully depending upon God for direction and insight.
Remember, we have no authority or power in the flesh. Satan can't do
anything about our position in Christ, but if he can get us to believe it
isn't true, we will live as though it's not.

Close with a prayer of thanksgiving for the authority and power you, a
believer, have in Christ Jesus.

6

JESUS HAS YOU COVERED

IDENTIFYING THE SOURCE

Frances asked, "How can I tell if my problems are in my mind, or the result of sin and disobedience against God, or the evidence of demonic influence?"

—What statement in Frances's letter (pages 101-102) is a clue that her problem was the result of demonic influence?

—What realization helped Frances to walk free?

GOD'S PROTECTION

What is Satan's role in the life of nonbelievers? (See 2 Corinthians 4:3-4.)

What is the deceiver's approach when a person turns his or her life over to God?

What do the germs in our world illustrate about how demons work and how we should deal with them?

What is the basis of our protection as Christians?

Passivity makes us vulnerable to attacks by Satan. Ephesians 6:10-18 outlines the protection that we as believers have in the Lord, and clearly states that we should not be passive. List the commands in verses 10-13 that demand action on our part.

DRESSED FOR BATTLE

According to Ephesians 6:14-17, what does the active-duty believer wear for protection?

What does Romans 13:14 say we are actually doing when we put on this armor?

What protection does this armor—this putting on of Christ—provide? (Look at John 14:30 and 1 John 5:18 for some additional thoughts about this.)

Armor You Have Already Put On

Look closely at Ephesians 6:14-15. Which pieces of armor did you put on when you first received Jesus Christ as Lord and Savior?

The Belt of Truth

—Why is this piece of armor important in the battle against Satan? (Consider how Jesus refers to Satan in John 8:44.)

—Mention two or three specific ways in which you can practice standing firm in the truth.

The Breastplate of Righteousness

—What does a breastplate do?

—What then does the breastplate of righteousness do?

—Standing firm in righteousness involves understanding and applying the principle of confession. How is confession different from saying, "I'm sorry" or asking for forgiveness?

—What does confession do in our lives?

The Shoes of Peace

—According to Romans 5:1, when we are justified by faith, we have peace with God. Why is peace with fellow believers important as well?

—Why would Satan be pleased with a lack of peace and unity among the children of God?

—What should be the basis for peace among believers?

The Rest of the Armor

The Shield of Faith

—Turn to Luke 4:1-13. How did Jesus deal with the devil's temptations?

—How are believers today to deal with the doubts, temptations, and accusations that Satan sends our way?

—How are you enlarging your shield of faith?

The Helmet of Salvation

—Spiritually speaking, why is it important that a Christian's head be protected?

—How does understanding our place in Christ help us to stand when under attack?

—What scriptures are especially powerful reminders that our salvation is secure for eternity?

The Sword of the Spirit

This refers to the written Word of God, and it is the only offensive weapon mentioned here.

—What common misconception do people have about Satan?

—Why is it important to speak out loud against Satan?

—What should our attitude of heart be when dealing with a satanic attack?

—What is significant about the order of the commands in James 4:7?

PRAYING BY THE SPIRIT

Ephesians 6:10-18 ends with a command to pray. Why is prayer important for taking a stand against Satan?

What instructions and information about prayer do the following verses give?

—Ephesians 6:18

—Romans 8:26

—Philippians 4:6

Take a few moments now to consider your prayer life. What is your attitude toward God when you pray? How regularly do you pray? Is the time you spend *speaking* balanced by time spent *listening*? How expectant and confident are your prayers? Write out a specific step you will take this week to improve your prayer life.

Combating Spiritual Blindness

What role can prayer play in the lives of people who have not yet recognized Jesus as Lord? Write out a two- or three-sentence evangelistic prayer that you can pray regularly on their behalf.

How can the spiritual sight of believers be improved? Again, write out a brief prayer that you can use for yourself and fellow believers.

Binding the Strong Man

According to Jesus's teaching in Matthew 12:29, what is the first step toward helping people become free of spiritual blindness and demonic influence?

Summarize C. Fred Dickason's guidelines for how to pray for a person being harassed by demons.

TAKING INVENTORY

What aspect of your spiritual armor needs "polishing"? Write out a plan for doing just that.

What were the two or three most striking things you learned about Satan and his ways in this chapter?

What did you learn about Christ and His provision to help you oppose Satan?

What has this chapter taught or reminded you about regarding evangelism and prayer for the lost?

How has this chapter helped you renew your commitment to prayer? What goal(s) have you set for yourself?

Look again at the larger scriptural context of the armor of God (Ephesians 6:10-21). What do you see as the foundation(s) for our use of the armor of God in our spiritual struggle?

PART TWO

STAND FIRM!

7

MANIPULATING SPIRITS

SHARON'S STORY

When Sharon sought help from a church that specialized in spiritual warfare, what approach did they take to help her?

What was the problem with this approach?

Read Isaiah 8:19-20. What does this scripture tell us as about dealing with spirits?

THE REBEL AUTHORITY

What action enabled Satan to take authority over the world—authority which he claimed in Luke 4:6?

What action changed the authority Satan had? Who now has the ultimate authority over heaven as well as earth? (See Matthew 28:18.)

When we received Christ, we became citizens of heaven (Philippians 3:20). Satan is the ruler of this world, but he is no longer our ruler—instead, Christ is our ruler. How does the Holy Spirit help us as we live on earth, Satan's turf? (See John 16:13.)

Degrees of Vulnerability

What is the difference between influence and ownership? Explain what Satan can and cannot do to believers.

The Powers That Be

Satan is a created being. He is not omnipresent, omniscient, or omnipotent. What do these facts about Satan suggest with regard to whether his emissaries—demons—exist?

Consider the "two equal and opposite errors" of disbelief and "unhealthy interest" in demons of which C.S. Lewis wrote. How can we counter these errors with the truth in our daily walk?

THE PERSONALITY OF DEMONS

Luke 11:24-26 offers the following insights into the personality and individuality of evil spirits.

1. Demons can exist outside or inside organic bodies.

2. They are able to travel at will.

3. They are able to communicate.

4. Each one has a separate and personal identity.

5. They are able to remember and make plans.

6. They are able to evaluate and make decisions.

7. They are able to combine forces.

8. They vary in degrees of wickedness.

—Which of these traits are new to you?

—How does this list of characteristics influence your perspective on demons? Do they seem more or less frightening? Why?

According to 1 John 4:4, why don't believers need to fear Satan?

According to what you know about the Bible and God's promises to His children, what are some other reasons believers don't need to fear Satan?

RUNNING THE GAUNTLET OF EVIL

Even when we walk in the light of Jesus Christ, evil spirits can interfere with our lives. Right now, think about your own walk down the street of row houses toward Jesus Christ. What have the beings inhabiting those houses been calling out to you?

"Hey, look over here! I've got something you really want. It tastes good, feels good, and is a lot more fun than your boring walk down the street. Come on in and take a look."

—What temptations are you most vulnerable to?

—How can God's Word help you stand strong? Write out a specific verse.

"Who do you think you are? God doesn't love you. You will never amount to anything. Surely you don't believe that bit about being saved." "See what you did! How can you call yourself a Christian when you behave like that?"

—What accusations are particularly defeating for you?

—Write out a specific verse from God's Word in response to each of the accusations you listed. (Consulting the list on pages 54-56 may help.)

"You don't need to go to church today. It's not important to pray and read the Bible every day. Some of the New Age stuff isn't so bad."

—Where does Satan try to deceive you about your walk with the Lord?

—What commands or encouragement from the Bible can keep you walking on the path you're called to?

In general, how does Satan try to make you slow down, stop, and even give up your journey toward Christ?

Having looked more closely at how Satan works, why do you think it is critical that Christians know the Bible?

RUNNING THE RACE

The text outlines three ways to respond to the demonic taunts and barbs being thrown at you from those second-story windows during your daily walk with Christ (see pages 127-129).

—Which two ways are wrong?

—Why are they wrong? More specifically, how do these actions conflict with what Scripture teaches?

What is the correct way to respond to harassment by demons?

What practical commands in Colossians 2:6-7 and 3:1-4 can keep you walking the road toward Christ?

A POSTSCRIPT

What, if anything, in this chapter did you find disturbing? Take time to review the passage in the book that was unsettling, then open your Bible to see how it answers your questions. Share your concerns with someone you trust and whose biblical understanding you respect. Do whatever is necessary to put your questions to rest so that Satan and his demons won't find a foothold of doubt in your mind.

What statements in this chapter were especially encouraging to you? Make a note of those that help provide the strength and courage you need to stand strong in Christ Jesus.

8

THE LURE OF KNOWLEDGE AND POWER

A TRAP AS OLD AS THE BIBLE

What is often the lure of the occult?

With what are we to satisfy our God-given desire for knowledge?

Look again at Moses's command to the children of Israel in Deuteronomy 18:9-13.

—Where do you see parallels with our world today?

—What can or should a Christian do in this situation?

—What does the information from our survey (see page 134) indicate about the appeal the occult has to Christians? About Christians' ignorance of the dangers of the occult?

KNOWLEDGE FROM THE DARK SIDE

Why do you think words from a psychic or a channeler are more appealing to people than what God has to say?

What do you think Satan is doing through today's psychics, channelers, palm readers, card readers, and other New Age practitioners? What is Satan's ultimate goal?

Charlatans and Real Mediums

Where do charlatans and real mediums get the information they share?

What differing goals do charlatans and real mediums have?

What is a believer's best defense against whatever appeal these fortune-tellers may have?

The Down Side of Seeking the Dark Side

How is the relationship between God's Spirit and Old Testament kings Saul and David different from the relationship between God's Spirit and New Testament believers today?

What do the following verses say about a believer's security?

—Ephesians 1:13-14

—John 10:28

—Romans 8:35-39

According to 1 Samuel 16:14, "The Spirit of the Lord departed from Saul, and an evil spirit from the Lord terrorized him." Why would God send an evil spirit to a person or nation?

What caused the evil spirit to leave Saul temporarily? (See 1 Samuel 16:23.)

What does this passage from Samuel suggest about the prominence of music in the spiritual realm?

What are the source and impact of much of today's popular secular music?

What warning is inherent in these facts?

Look again at the account of the rich man and Lazarus in Luke 16:19-31.

—What does this story teach about the possibility of the living communicating with the dead?

—In light of this teaching, how are believers to regard psychics who claim contact with the dead, psychologists who claim to regress a client back to a former existence, and New Age mediums who purport to channel a person from the past into the present?

An Old Idea in New Clothing

How is Satan the deceiver at work in the New Age movement? Consider some of the New Age watchwords and catchphrases.

How is today's New Age situation similar to the times of the early church and even the world of our Hebrew ancestors?

—Acts 8:9-10

—Acts 16:16-18

—Leviticus 17:7

—Psalm 106:36-38

—Deuteronomy 32:15-18

—1 Timothy 4:1

Even believers are vulnerable to being lured away by the counterfeit knowledge and power of our enemy, who exaggerates our sense of independence and importance apart from God. How can we, who are God's children, protect ourselves in this area?

A POSTSCRIPT

What, if anything, in this chapter did you find disturbing? Take time to review the passage in the book that was unsettling, then open your Bible to see how it answers your questions. Share your concerns with someone you trust and whose biblical understanding you respect. Do whatever is necessary to put your questions to rest so that Satan and his demons won't find a foothold of doubt in your mind.

What statements in this chapter were especially encouraging? Make a note of those that help provide the strength and courage you need to stand strong in Christ Jesus.

9

TEMPTED TO DO IT YOUR WAY

TEMPTATION AND SIN

Does the fact that a person is bombarded by tempting thoughts mean that he or she is a sinner? Why or why not?

How is sin different from temptation?

Does temptation automatically lead to sin? Explain your answer.

Read Hebrews 4:16. What resource do we have in time of temptation?

Write out the promise of 1 Corinthians 10:13 and memorize this powerful verse.

THE BASIS OF TEMPTATION

What characterizes the life of a person who is spiritually dead?

According to the text, what are we tempted to look to in order to meet our basic needs?

Why is this so?

Read Philippians 4:19. What does this verse teach about what God will do for His people?

What determines the power of temptation in a person's life?

Too Much of a Good Thing

How do you define "sin"?

Look again at the ways good can become sin:

physical rest becomes laziness

quietness becomes noncommunication

ability to profit becomes avarice and greed

enjoyment of life becomes intemperance

physical pleasure becomes sensuality

admiring what others possess becomes covetousness

enjoyment of food becomes gluttony

self-care becomes vanity

self-respect becomes conceit

communication becomes gossip

cautiousness becomes unbelief

positiveness becomes insensitivity

anger becomes rage and bad temper

lovingkindness becomes overprotection

judgment becomes criticism

same-sex friendship becomes homosexuality

sexual freedom becomes immorality

conscientiousness becomes perfectionism

generosity becomes wastefulness

self-protection becomes dishonesty

carefulness becomes fear

—Which items on this list warn you of potential areas of sin in your life?

—Take those areas of concern before the Lord in prayer right now.

What new understanding of sin do this list and the discussion on pages 151-154 offer you?

Sin Versus Growth

Turn in your Bible to 1 John 2. According to verses 12-14, what characterizes the following three stages of Christian growth?

—"little children"

—"young men"

—"fathers"

Which stage do you perceive you are in right now?

What are you doing to ensure your continuing growth in Christ?

CHANNELS OF TEMPTATION

According to 1 John 2:16, what are the three channels through which Satan will entice you to act independently of God?

Describe the three channels of temptation you just listed.

The Lust of the Flesh

Satan watched Jesus fast for 40 days and concluded that His hunger might be a point of vulnerability. What other soft spots of vulnerability does Satan look for in believers?

In Matthew 4:1-11, Jesus modeled a way of resisting Satan's temptations. He countered the temptations with the Word of God—the source of life we can draw on for strength. What truth did Jesus claim in Matthew 4:4 in response to Satan's appeal to the lust of the flesh?

The Lust of the Eyes

How can the things we see weaken our confidence in God?

What is wrong and dangerous about a "prove it to me" attitude?

What truth did Jesus claim in Matthew 4:7?

The Pride of Life

How did Satan use the pride of life to become the god of this world?

Satan offered Jesus the kingdoms of the world just as he had offered them to Adam and Eve. In response, what truth did Jesus claim in Matthew 4:10?

There are three critical issues reflected in these channels of temptation we have just looked at: (1) the *will of God*, as expressed through your *dependence on God*; (2) the *Word of God*, as expressed through your *confidence in God*; and (3) the *worship of God*, as expressed through your humble *obedience to God*. Be aware!

TWO OF OUR BIGGEST APPETITES

Temptation's hook is the devil's promise that what we think we want and need outside God's will can satisfy us. In reality, what is the only thing that can truly satisfy our heart's desires?

Eat to Live or Live to Eat? Food is necessary for survival and basic physical health. What are some unnatural reasons people turn to food? Do you find yourself turning to food for any of those reasons? If so, consider the spiritual dimension of that action and take your struggle to the Lord in prayer.

Sexual Passions Unleashed. Sex is a natural, God-given part of life, but it is also a powerful temptation to sin. Why is sexual sin unique and so dangerous? See Romans 6:12-13 and 1 Corinthians 6:18. If Satan is using sex to tempt you to stray from God and the path He calls you to, remember to address the spiritual dimension of that temptation.

THE WAY OF ESCAPE

Turn to 2 Corinthians 10:5 and look at the second part of that verse. What is the first step for escaping temptation when a tempting thought enters your mind?

The second step for standing strong against temptation is to evaluate the thought that Satan has planted in your mind. Turn to Philippians 4:8. List the eightfold criterion for what believers should think about.

What should a believer do with a thought that fails the test of God's Word, a thought that doesn't meet the standards listed in Philippians 4:8?

Confession and resisting the devil comprise an important step of escape. What does James 4:7 promise about the effectiveness of this step?

Consider what you've learned about Satan. How can you better resist sin when the devil plants tempting thoughts in your mind?

A POSTSCRIPT

Was anything in this chapter disturbing to you? Do whatever is biblically necessary to put your questions to rest so that Satan and his demons won't find a foothold of doubt in your mind.

What statements in this chapter were especially encouraging to you? Make a note of those which help provide the strength and courage you need to stand strong in Christ Jesus.

10

ACCUSED BY THE FATHER OF LIES

SATAN'S ACCUSATIONS

Why are accusations effective weapons in Satan's battle against the kingdom of God? In other words, what do accusations keep believers from doing?

Why are accusations a powerful follow-up to the temptations that believers give in to?

What accusations does Satan frequently use against you?

Write out a verse from Scripture to counter each one of those lies.

PUTTING THE ACCUSER IN HIS PLACE

Zechariah 3:1-10 shows how God responds to our accuser. This teaches us an important truth about how we can stand strong against Satan's accusations.

The Lord Rebukes Satan

In the scene described in Zechariah 3:1-3, what is Satan doing?

What does God say in response to Satan's words?

Imagine an earthly parallel to this courtroom scene. How can you effectively respond to Satan's accusing words?

The Lord Removes Our Filthy Garments

Why are Satan's accusations groundless? Think about the cross of Christ.

Who removes our unrighteousness?

Why is it important to remember that we, in ourselves, don't have any garments of righteousness to put on that will satisfy God?

The Lord Admonishes Us to Respond

God rebukes Satan and clothes us in righteousness. How does He want us to respond? (See Zechariah 3:7.)

What are some practical ways you can serve God and live out your identity in Christ? Be specific.

RECOGNIZING A CRITICAL DIFFERENCE

The devil's accusations and the Holy Spirit's convictions both cause sorrow, but that sorrow can go in two different directions. Where do Satan's accusations lead? And where do the Holy Spirit's convictions lead?

How can you determine whether you are being falsely accused? What feelings and thoughts about yourself will you have if Satan is the one causing your sorrow?

What truth about sorrow do you see illustrated in the contrasting life stories of Judas Iscariot and Simon Peter?

Read the following verses and compare the work of Satan with the work of Jesus Christ.

—Revelation 12:10—The work of Satan:

—Hebrews 7:25—The work of Jesus:

THE QUICKSAND OF ACCUSATION

What can happen if we refuse to take a stand against the accuser?

Satan will tell believers lies about their worth. We are to ignore those lies and, instead, believe what God says about us. What does God say about you? Write out the following scriptures, plus any others you think of. These words of truth are words of freedom that can keep you from sinking in the quicksand of Satan's accusations.

—Romans 5:8

—1 John 3:1

—Psalm 139

—1 John 1:9

—Romans 8:38-39

Read Romans 8:31-39 and answer the following questions.

—Someone is against us, but it can't be God. Why not?

—Who will bring a charge against God's elect? It can't be God. Why not?

—Who is the one who condemns? It can't be Jesus. Why not?

—Who can separate you from the love of God?

THE UNPARDONABLE SIN

What are the sources of a believer's fear that he or she has committed the unpardonable sin?

Which piece of our spiritual armor does this fear weaken?

Look again at Mark 3:22-30. How do we know from Jesus's teaching that a believer cannot commit the unpardonable sin?

The devil can mislead us, discourage us, and accuse us of something we've never done. What might our questioning of "authorities" be, since we know that it cannot be blasphemy of the Holy Spirit? (See 1 John 4:1-6.)

A POSTSCRIPT

Was anything in this chapter disturbing to you? Do whatever is necessary to put your questions to rest so that Satan and his demons won't find a foothold of doubt in your mind.

What statements in this chapter were especially encouraging? Make a note of those that help provide the strength and courage you need to stand strong in Christ Jesus.

11

THE DANGER OF DECEPTION

SATAN'S NUMBER ONE STRATEGY

Satan will attempt to dissuade believers through self-deception, false prophets/teachers, and deceiving spirits. What aspects of your spiritual armor need to be ready to do battle?

BEWARE OF SELF-DECEPTION

The Scriptures reveal several patterns of behavior through which Christians become vulnerable to self-deception.

We deceive ourselves when we hear the Word of God but don't do it.

—What are we commanded in James 1:22 and 2:14-20?

—If you are a preacher or teacher, ask yourself: Does your life always measure up to the passage of Scripture you are sharing? If not, what should this inconsistency compel you to do?

—When you receive the Word through another person's teaching, do you faithfully put it into practice? Why or why not?

—What should a believer's life model instead of perfectionism?

—Why would honesty in a Christian community—honesty about struggles, failures, and sins—discourage Satan and his demons?

We deceive ourselves when we say we have no sin.

—What does Romans 3:23 teach about sinfulness?

—What does 1 John 1:8 add to that teaching?

—Why is it important to confess and deal with sin on a daily basis?

We deceive ourselves when we think we are something we are not.

—By what and whose standards should we as believers evaluate ourselves?

—What cautions do Romans 12:3 and Galatians 6:3 offer?

—Who is the source of all your goodness? Who, then, should receive the credit for any goodness in you?

We deceive ourselves when we possess worldly wisdom yet lack an eternal perspective.

—What do the following verses teach about real wisdom?

1 Corinthians 2:16

1 Corinthians 3:18-19

Proverbs 3:5-6

Job 42:1-2

Psalm 111:10

—Think about today's world. In what ways does the "wisdom" of the world reflect immoral, ungodly, and humanistic values? List some examples:

—How can you keep yourself standing strong in God's values?

We deceive ourselves when we think we are mature but can't control what we say.

—What does Scripture teach about the power of the tongue?

James 1:26

Luke 6:45

Ephesians 4:29

James 3:5-12

Proverbs 10:19

—How, then, does our tongue reflect our devotion or lack of devotion to God?

We deceive ourselves when we think we will face no consequences for our behavior.

—What can result from the seeds we sow in this life?

Galatians 6:7-10

Proverbs 22:8

Hosea 10:12-13

2 Corinthians 9:6

Luke 6:38

—God forgives our sins, but He doesn't necessarily spare us from the consequences of our sinful acts. Can you recall times when God has taught you this lesson? Be specific.

We deceive ourselves when we think the unrighteous will inherit the kingdom of God.

—What does 1 Corinthians 6:9-10 teach about who will not inherit the kingdom of God?

—What does James 2:14-19,22,26 teach about how a believer's life should reflect his or her faith?

We deceive ourselves when we think we can continually associate with bad company and not be corrupted.

—What do Proverbs 22:24-25 and 1 Corinthians 15:33 teach regarding the importance of the company we keep?

—When have you seen the truth of this teaching in your own life or the life of someone you care about?

—Do these biblical teachings prohibit ministry to the amoral or immoral people of the world? Explain.

BEWARE OF FALSE PROPHETS AND TEACHERS

Compare the Counterfeit with the Real

—Criterion #1: What effect do the words of true prophecy have on those who hear them? (See Jeremiah 23:22.)

—Criterion #2: What is the ultimate authority guiding a true prophet's message? (See Jeremiah 23:25-28.)

—Criterion #3: What is the effect of a prophecy from the Lord? (See Jeremiah 23:29.)

—Criterion #4: What phrase can tip you off to an act of plagiarism by a so-called prophet? Why wouldn't God use a person in this way?

Signs and Wonders: Who's Being Tested?

—What guideline does Deuteronomy 18:22 offer?

—Now look at Deuteronomy 13:1-3; Matthew 24:23-25; and Mark 13:22. What is the purpose of false signs and wonders?

—An occurrence of the miraculous does not necessarily mean the presence of God. What can a believer do to test all signs, wonders, and dreams?

Counterfeits in the Church

—In his second epistle, Peter warns about false prophets and teachers who operate within the church. What will they do? (See 2 Peter 2:1.)

—Although the biblical criteria for evaluating ministry are truth and righteousness, how will false teachers in the church lead you to evaluate their ministry? (See 2 Peter 2:2 and page 182 of the text.)

—What are two characteristics of false prophets? (See 2 Peter 2:10.)

—What should Christians in leadership roles be willing to do to ensure that false teaching does not arise within the church? How closely does your church follow the biblical teachings on church leadership?

BEWARE OF DECEIVING SPIRITS

What warnings do the following Scripture passages offer?

—1 Timothy 4:1

—1 John 2:18

—1 John 4:1-6

What did Hannah Whithall Smith's perspective, as stated on page 183 of the text, teach you about demons?

What major points should be included in a prayer for freedom from deceiving spirits? (Note: An example is given on pages 183-184.)

SPIRITUAL DISCERNMENT

What is the correct motive for true spiritual discernment?

Spiritual discernment is not a mere function of the mind. What is it a function of? Explain.

Why is discernment an important gift to individual believers and to the church in general?

A POSTSCRIPT

Was anything in this chapter disturbing to you? Do whatever is necessary to put your questions to rest so that Satan and his demons won't find a foothold of doubt in your mind.

What statements in this chapter were especially encouraging? Make a note of those that help provide the strength and courage you need to stand strong in Christ Jesus.

PART THREE

WALK FREE!

12

HELPING OTHERS

KINGDOMS IN CONFLICT

Satanic intrusion does not mean satanic ownershp. How does Romans 8:35-39 support this truth?

Even though he can never own a believer, how does Satan seem to control a believer's life?

Why does the English term "demon possessed" sometimes lead to confusion?

A struggling Christian is like a house filled to overflowing with garbage that attracts flies. What is the typical knee-jerk response from such a Christian? What is the right response?

When it comes to living the Christian life, we have to understand what God's role is, and what our role is. What is God's role, and what is ours?

From the standpoint of human responsibility, what does God expect of us according to 2 Timothy 2:15 and Romans 12:3?

Some Christians question God's presence in their lives and His love for them. But what has God already done on our behalf to help us? And whose responsibility is it to submit to God and resist the devil?

WHO IS RESPONSIBLE FOR WHAT?

When it comes to helping someone, three parties need to be present: God, the encourager, and the inquirer. What is likely to happen when we leave God out of the picture?

"There is a sovereign role that God and only God can play in the life of another, and we will foul up the process if we usurp His role." Do you agree or disagree with that statement? Why?

When helping someone who is dealing with a problem, why does it make sense to first make sure that person is in a right relationship with God?

A POSTSCRIPT

When it comes to putting on our spiritual protection, what acts of responsibility are outlined for each believer in these now-familiar passages?

—Romans 13:14

—2 Corinthians 10:5

—Romans 6:12

—James 4:7

Was anything in this chapter disturbing to you? Do whatever is necessary to put your questions to rest so that Satan and his demons won't find a foothold of doubt in your mind.

What statements in this chapter were especially encouraging? Make a note of those that help provide the strength and courage you need to stand strong in Christ Jesus.

THE STEPS TO FREEDOM IN CHRIST

Remember, you are a child of God and seated with Christ in the heavenlies (the spiritual realm). That means you have the authority and power to do His will. The Steps don't set you free. Jesus sets you free, and you will progressively experience that freedom as you respond to Him in faith and repentance.

Successfully completing this repentance process is not an end; it is the beginning of growth. Unless any sin issues are resolved, however, the growth process will be stalled, and your Christian life will remain stagnant.

With these Steps, ultimately the purpose is to become firmly rooted in Christ. Keep in mind there is no such thing as instant maturity; renewing your mind and conforming to the image of God is a lifelong process.

—————————————— **STEP 1:** ——————————————

Counterfeit Versus Real

Renounce your past or present involvements with occult practices and cult teachings and rituals, as well as non-Christian religions.

Complete the "Non-Christian Spiritual Experience Inventory" on pages 217-218 of the text. If you don't have the book, ask God to help you list all your involvements with occult practices and cult teachings and rituals, as well as non-Christian religions.

Pray the following prayer:

> *Dear heavenly Father, please bring to my mind anything and everything that I have done knowingly or unknowingly that involves occultic, cultic, or false religious teachings and practices. Grant me the wisdom and grace to renounce any and all spiritual counterfeits, false religious teachings and practices. In Jesus's name I pray. Amen.*

Once you have completed your checklist and the questions, confess and renounce *each* item you were involved in by praying the following prayer *out loud*:

> *Dear heavenly Father, I confess that I have participated in [specifically name every belief and involvement with all that you have checked on the "Non-Christian Spiritual Experience Inventory"], and I renounce them all as counterfeits. I pray that You will fill me with Your Holy Spirit so that I may be guided by You. Thank You that in Christ, I am forgiven. Amen.*

--- **STEP 2** ---

Deception Versus Truth

Accept and believe the truth of God's Word in the innermost part of your being. Lay aside falsehood and deception.

Look at John 14:6; 16:13; and 17:17; as well as Ephesians 4:14-16.

—What do these verses say about truth with regard to the persons of the Godhead?

—What specifically does Ephesians 4:14-16 say about truth in relationships?

In Psalm 32:2, what did David write about living without deceit?

What do you think "blessed" would mean to you in your experience of walking in the truth?

Where does the strength to "walk in the Light" (1 John 1:7) come from?

Pray the following prayer:

Dear heavenly Father, You are the truth, and I desire to live by faith according to Your truth. The truth will set me free, but in many ways I have been deceived by the father of lies, the philosophies of this fallen world, and even by myself. I choose

> *to walk in the light, knowing that You love and accept me just*
> *as I am. As I consider areas of possible deception, I invite the*
> *Spirit of truth to guide me into all truth. Please protect me*
> *from all deception as You "search me, O God, and know my*
> *heart; try me and know my anxious thoughts; and see if there*
> *be any hurtful way in me, and lead me in the everlasting way"*
> *(Psalm 139:23-24). In the name of Jesus I pray. Amen.*

As you go through the checklist titled "Ways You Can Be Deceived by the World" on pages 221-222 and list the areas that apply to your life, take the time to look up the scriptures and think about them. Whether or not you have a copy of *The Bondage Breaker*, pray to God that He would bring to your memory those things you need to write down.

For each deception, pray this prayer of confession:

> *Dear heavenly Father, I confess that I have deceived myself*
> *by [confess the item]. Thank You for Your forgiveness. I com-*
> *mit myself to believing only Your truth. In Jesus's name I pray.*
> *Amen.*

Work through the checklist titled "Ways to Deceive Yourself" on page 223. Again, if you don't have *The Bondage Breaker*, write down the kinds of deceptions God brings to your mind. Take the time to look up relevant scriptures and think about them.

Pray this prayer of confession for each deception you need to renounce:

> *Lord, I confess that I have deceived myself by _____ .*
> *Thank You for Your forgiveness. I commit myself to believing*
> *only Your truth. In Jesus's name. Amen.*

Complete the checklist "Ways to Wrongly Defend Yourself" on page 224. If you do not have a copy of *The Bondage Breaker*, do what you can and ask the Lord to help you write down the things that are necessary for you to confess.

Use this prayer to confess these sins:

> *Dear heavenly Father, I confess that I have wrongly defended myself by [confess the items checked on the list]. Thank You for Your forgiveness. I trust You to defend and protect me. In Jesus's name I pray. Amen.*

What do we need to learn about the lies we have used to defend ourselves?

What must we recognize about faith?

Read aloud the following Statements of Truth. You may find it helpful to read these statements daily for several weeks so you can renew your mind with the truth and replace any lies you may be believing.

——————— STATEMENTS OF TRUTH ———————

1. *I recognize* that there is only one true and living God who exists as the Father, Son, and Holy Spirit. He is worthy of all honor, praise, and glory as the One who made all things and holds all things together. (See Exodus 20:2-3; Colossians 1:16-17.)

2. *I recognize* that Jesus Christ is the Messiah, the Word who became flesh and dwelt among us. I believe that He came to destroy the works of the devil, and that He disarmed the rulers and authorities and made a public display of them, having triumphed over them. (See John 1:1,14; Colossians 2:15; 1 John 3:8.)

3. *I believe* that God demonstrated His own love for me in that while

I was still a sinner, Christ died for me. I believe that He has delivered me from the domain of darkness and transferred me to His kingdom, and in Him I have redemption, the forgiveness of sins. (See Romans 5:8; Colossians 1:13-14.)

4. *I believe* that I am now a child of God and that I am seated with Christ in the heavenly realms. I believe that I was saved by the grace of God through faith, and that it was a gift and not a result of any works on my part. (See Ephesians 2:6,8-9; 1 John 3:1-3.)

5. *I choose* to be strong in the Lord and in the strength of His might. I put no confidence in the flesh, for the weapons of warfare are not of the flesh but are divinely powerful for the destruction of strongholds. I put on the full armor of God. I resolve to stand firm in my faith and resist the evil one. (See 2 Corinthians 10:4; Ephesians 6:10-20; Philippians 3:3.)

6. *I believe* that apart from Christ I can do nothing, so I declare my complete dependence on Him. I choose to abide in Christ in order to bear much fruit and glorify my Father. I announce to Satan that Jesus is my Lord. I reject any and all counterfeit gifts or works of Satan in my life. (See John 15:5,8; 1 Corinthians 12:3.)

7. *I believe* that the truth will set me free and that Jesus is the truth. If He sets me free, I will be free indeed. I recognize that walking in the light is the only path of true fellowship with God and man. Therefore, I stand against all of Satan's deceptions by taking every thought captive in obedience to Christ. I declare that the Bible is the only authoritative standard for truth and life. (See John 8:32,36; 14:6; 2 Corinthians 10:5; 2 Timothy 3:15-17; 1 John 1:3-7.)

8. *I choose* to present my body to God as a living and holy sacrifice and the members of my body as instruments of righteousness. I choose to renew my mind by the living Word of God in order that I may prove that the will of God is good, acceptable, and perfect. I put off the old

self with its evil practices and put on the new self. I declare myself to be a new creation in Christ. (See Romans 6:13; 12:1-2; 2 Corinthians 5:17; Colossians 3:9-10.)

9. *By faith I choose* to be filled with the Spirit so that I can be guided into all truth. I choose to walk by the Spirit so that I will not carry out the desires of the flesh. (See John 16:13; Galatians 5:16; Ephesians 5:18.)

10. *I renounce* all selfish goals and choose the ultimate goal of love. I choose to obey the two greatest commandments: to love the Lord my God with all my heart, soul, mind, and strength, and to love my neighbor as myself. (See Matthew 22:37-39; 1 Timothy 1:5.)

11. *I believe* that the Lord Jesus has all authority in heaven and on earth, and He is the head over all rule and authority. I am complete in Him. I believe that Satan and his demons are subject to me in Christ because I am a member of Christ's body. Therefore, I obey the command to submit to God and resist the devil, and I command Satan, in the name of Jesus Christ, to leave my presence. (See Matthew 28:18; Ephesians 1:19-23; Colossians 2:10; James 4:7.)

STEP 3:

Bitterness Versus Forgiveness

Forgive others as you have been forgiven for your sin through Jesus's death on the cross (Ephesians 4:31-32).

Ask God to bring to your mind the people you need to forgive by praying the following prayer out loud:

> *Dear heavenly Father, I thank You for the riches of Your kindness, forbearance, and patience toward me, knowing that Your kindness has led me to repentance. I confess that I have not shown that same kindness and patience towards those who*

have hurt or offended me (Romans 2:4). Instead, I have held on to my anger, bitterness, and resentment toward them. Please bring to my mind all the people I need to forgive in order that I may now do so. In Jesus's name I pray. Amen.

On a separate sheet of paper, list the names of people who come to your mind. At this point, don't question whether you need to forgive them or not. If a name comes to mind, just write it down.

Often we hold things against ourselves as well, punishing ourselves for wrong choices we've made in the past. Write "myself" at the bottom of your list so you can forgive yourself.

Also write "thoughts against God" at the bottom of your list. Obviously, God has never done anything wrong, so He doesn't need our forgiveness. Sometimes, however, we harbor angry thoughts against Him because He did not do what we wanted Him to do. Those feelings of anger or resentment against God can become a wall between us and Him, so we must let them go.

What does forgetting have to do with forgiving?

Is forgiveness a matter of the will or the emotions? Explain.

—What does holding on to the right to revenge do to us?

—How is forgiveness an act of trust in God?

—How does a person who forgives benefit from that act?

Do we benefit from forgiveness even if we have to live with the consequences of someone else's sin? Explain.

Work through your list of people to forgive. Starting with the first person on your list, make the choice to forgive him or her for every painful memory that comes to your mind. Stay with that individual until you are sure you have dealt with all the remembered pain. Then work your way down the list and do the same with the other people.

As you do this, God may bring to your mind painful memories you've long forgotten. Let Him do this even if it hurts. God wants you to be free; forgiving those people is the only way. Don't try to excuse the offender's behavior, even if it is someone you are close to.

Don't say, "Lord, please help me to forgive." He is already helping you and will be with you all the way through the process. Don't say, "Lord, I *want* to forgive…" because that bypasses the hard choice you have to make to extend forgiveness. Rather, say, "Lord, I *choose* to forgive…"

For every painful memory that God reveals in connection with each person on your list, pray out loud,

> *Dear heavenly Father, I choose to forgive [name the person] for [what they did or failed to do], because it made me feel [share the painful feelings—i.e., rejected, dirty, worthless, inferior, etc.].*

After you have forgiven each person for all the offenses that came to your mind, and after you have honestly expressed how you felt, conclude your forgiveness of that person by praying out loud,

> *Lord Jesus, I choose not to hold on to my resentment. I relinquish my right to seek revenge and ask You to heal my damaged*

*emotions. Thank You for setting me free from the bondage of
my bitterness. I now ask You to bless those who have hurt me.
In Jesus's name I pray. Amen.*

STEP 4:

Rebellion Versus Submission

It is easy to believe the lie that those in authority over us are only robbing us of the freedom to do what we want. The truth is that God has
placed them there for our protection and liberty. Rebelling against
God and the authorities He has set up is a serious sin, for it gives Satan
a wide-open avenue for attack. Submission is the only solution. God
requires more, however, than just the outward appearance of submission; He wants us to sincerely submit from the heart. Rebelling against
God and His established authorities leaves us spiritually vulnerable.

What are our biblical responsibilities with regard to authority?

What do the following passages teach about submission to authority?

—Romans 13:1-5

—1 Timothy 2:1-4

—1 Peter 2:13-16

—1 Peter 2:18-21

—1 Peter 3:1-2

—Ephesians 6:1-3

—Hebrews 13:17

How is submission to human authority an act of faith?

What is the only exception to the biblical command to submit to human authority? (See Acts 4:19 and 5:29.)

Pray as you look over the list on page 235. Look up the scriptures you haven't already thought upon, and list the specific ways in which you have been rebellious toward authorities. Ask God to help you remember the things you need to write down, even if you don't have a copy of *The Bondage Breaker*.

Use the following prayer to specifically confess these sins:

> *Heavenly Father, I confess that I have been rebellious toward [name or position] by [specifically confess what you did or did not do]. Thank You for Your forgiveness. I choose to be submissive and obedient to Your Word. In Jesus's name I pray. Amen.*

STEP 5:
Pride Versus Humility

Let go of pride, which says, "I don't need God or anyone else," and humble yourself before your heavenly Father and sovereign Lord.

Why is pride so deadly to one's spiritual life?

According to Philippians 3:3, what is a good definition of humility?

What instructions do the following passages give?

—James 4:6-10

—1 Peter 5:1-10

Use the following prayer to express your commitment to living humbly before God:

> *Dear heavenly Father, You have said that pride goes before destruction and an arrogant spirit before stumbling. I confess that I have focused on my own needs and desires and not those of others. I have not always denied myself, picked up my cross daily, and followed You. I have relied on my own strength and resources instead of resting in Yours. I have placed my will before Yours and centered my life around myself instead of You. I confess my pride and selfishness and pray that all ground gained in my life by the enemies of the Lord Jesus Christ would be canceled as I repent and overcome these sinful flesh patterns.*

I choose to rely upon the Holy Spirit's power and guidance so that I will do nothing from selfishness or empty conceit. With humility of mind, I choose to regard others as more important than myself. I acknowledge You as my Lord, and confess that apart from You I can do nothing of lasting significance. Please examine my heart and show me the specific ways I have lived my life in pride. In the gentle and humble name of Jesus I pray. Amen. (See Proverbs 16:18; Matthew 6:33; 16:24; Romans 12:10; Philippians 2:3.)

Having made this commitment in prayer, allow God to show you any specific ways in which you have lived in a proud manner, using the list on page 237. If you don't have a copy of *The Bondage Breaker*, do your best to be as thorough as God enables you to be.

For each area of pride you need to confess, pray out loud,

Lord, I agree I have been proud in [name the area]. Thank You for forgiving me for my pride. I choose to humble myself before You and others. I choose to place all my confidence in You and none in my flesh. In Jesus's name I pray. Amen.

STEP 6:

Bondage Versus Freedom

To find freedom from the vicious cycle of "sin-confess, sin-confess," we must follow James 4:7, which tells us to submit to God and resist the devil.

How can other believers help you if you feel trapped by habitual sin? (See James 5:16.)

Whom can you call on to pray for and with you? Do so.

How can you be sure God will forgive you for your sin? Write out the promise of 1 John 1:9, and replace the "we," "us," and "our" with "I," "me," and "my."

Pray the following prayer out loud:

> *Dear heavenly Father, You have told me to put on the Lord Jesus Christ and make no provision for the flesh in regard to its lusts. I confess that I have given in to fleshly lusts that wage war against my soul. I thank You that in Christ my sins are already forgiven, but I have broken Your holy law and I have allowed sin to wage war in my body. I come to You now to confess and renounce these sins of the flesh so that I might be cleansed and set free from the bondage of sin. Please reveal to my mind all the sins of the flesh I have committed and the ways I have grieved the Holy Spirit. In Jesus's holy name I pray. Amen.* (See Romans 6:12-13; 13:14; 2 Corinthians 4:2; James 4:1; 1 Peter 2:11; 5:8.)

There are many sins of the flesh that can control us. Open your Bible to Mark 7:20-23; Galatians 5:19-21; and Ephesians 4:25-31 and pray through these verses, asking the Lord to reveal the specific ways you have sinned. Use the checklist on page 240 of *The Bondage Breaker* as well, if you have the book available, to make as complete a record as possible of those things you need to confess.

Confess each of these sins by praying:

> *Dear heavenly Father, I confess that I have sinned against You by [name the sins]. Thank You for Your forgiveness and*

cleansing. I now turn away from these expressions of sin and turn to You, Lord. Fill me with Your Holy Spirit so that I will not carry out the desires of the flesh. In Jesus's name I pray. Amen.

It is our responsibility to not allow sin to have control over our bodies. We must not use our bodies or another person's body as an instrument of unrighteousness (Romans 6:12-13).

Read 1 Corinthians 6:15-20 and give two reasons that sexual immorality is an especially serious matter.

Dwell on Romans 6:12-13 and 1 Corinthians 6:15-20 as you allow God to bring to your mind those sexual sins you want freedom from. Pray this prayer:

Dear heavenly Father, I have allowed sin to reign in my mortal body. I ask You to bring to my mind every sexual use of my body as an instrument of unrighteousness so that I can renounce these sexual sins and break these sinful bondages. In Jesus's name I pray. Amen.

As the Lord brings to your mind every sexually immoral use of your body, whether it was done to you (rape, incest, sexual molestation) or you initiated it (pornography, masturbation, sexual immorality), renounce these using the prayer that follows:

Dear heavenly Father, I renounce [name the sexual experience] with [name]. I ask You to break that sinful bond with [name] spiritually, physically, and emotionally. In Jesus's name I pray. Amen.

After you are finished, commit your body to the Lord by praying,

Dear heavenly Father, I renounce all the uses of my body as an instrument of unrighteousness, and I admit to any willful

participation. I choose to present my physical body to You as an instrument of righteousness, a living and holy sacrifice acceptable to You. I choose to reserve the sexual use of my body for marriage only. I reject the devil's lie that my body is not clean or that it is dirty or in any way unacceptable to You as a result of my past sexual experiences. Lord, thank You that You have cleansed and forgiven me and that You love and accept me just the way I am. Therefore, I choose now to accept myself and my body as clean in Your eyes. In Jesus's name I pray. Amen. (See Hebrews 13:4.)

Special Prayers and Decisions for Specific Situations

If the Lord has brought to your mind a special need, use one of the prayers below to confess your sin, renounce deception, and claim your freedom in Christ.

Marriage

Dear heavenly Father, I choose to believe that You created us male and female, and that marriage is a spiritual bond between one man and one woman who become one in Christ. I believe that bond can be broken only by death, adultery, or desertion by an unbelieving spouse. I choose to stay committed to my vows and to remain faithful to my spouse until physical death separates us. Give me the grace to be the spouse You created me to be, and enable me to love and respect my partner in marriage. I will seek to change only myself and accept my spouse as You have accepted me. Teach me how to speak the truth in love, to be merciful as You have been merciful to me, and to forgive as You have forgiven me. In Jesus's name I pray. Amen.

Divorce

Dear heavenly Father, I have not been the spouse You created me to be, and I deeply regret that my marriage has failed. I choose to believe that You still love and accept me. I choose to believe that I am still Your child, and that Your desire for me is that I continue serving You and others in Your kingdom. Give me the grace to overcome the disappointment and the emotional scars that I carry, and I ask the same for my ex-spouse. I choose to forgive him/her and to forgive myself for all the ways I contributed to the divorce. Enable me to learn from my mistakes and guide me so that I don't repeat the same old flesh patterns. I choose to believe the truth that I am still accepted, secure, and significant in Christ. Please guide me to healthy relationships in Your church, and keep me from seeking a marriage on the rebound. I trust You to supply all my needs in the future, and I commit myself to following You. In Jesus's name I pray. Amen.

Gender Identity

Dear heavenly Father, I choose to believe that You have created all humanity to be either male or female (Genesis 1:27) and commanded us to maintain a distinction between the two genders (Deuteronomy 22:5; Romans 1:24-29). I confess that I have been influenced by the social pressures of this fallen world and the lies of Satan to question my biological gender identity and that of others. I renounce all the accusations and lies of Satan that would seek to convince me that I am somebody other than who You created me to be. I choose to believe and accept my biological gender identity, and pray that You would heal my damaged emotions and enable me to be transformed by the renewing of my mind. I take up the full armor of God (Ephesians 6:13-17) and the shield of faith to extinguish all the temptations and accusations of the evil one (Ephesians 6:16). I renounce any identities and labels that derive from my old nature, and I choose to believe that I am a new creation in Christ. In the wonderful name of Jesus I pray. Amen.

Abortion

Dear heavenly Father, I confess that I was not a proper guardian and keeper of the life You entrusted to me, and I confess that I have sinned. Thank You that because of Your forgiveness, I can forgive myself. I commit the child to You for all eternity, and believe that he or she is in Your caring hands. In Jesus's name I pray. Amen.

Suicidal Tendencies

Dear heavenly Father, I renounce all suicidal thoughts and any attempts I've made to take my own life or in any way injure myself. I renounce the lie that life is hopeless and that I can find peace and freedom by taking my own life. Satan is a thief and comes to steal, kill, and destroy. I choose to remain alive in Christ, who said He came to give me life and give it abundantly. Thank You for Your forgiveness that allows me to forgive myself. I choose to believe that there is always hope in Christ and that my heavenly Father loves me. In Jesus's name I pray. Amen.

Drivenness and Perfectionism

Dear heavenly Father, I renounce the lie that my sense of worth is dependent upon my ability to perform. I announce the truth that my identity and sense of worth are found in who I am as Your child. I renounce seeking the approval and acceptance of other people for my affirmation, and I choose to believe the truth that I am already approved and accepted in Christ because of His death and resurrection for me. I choose to believe the truth that I have been saved not by deeds done in righteousness, but according to Your mercy. I choose to believe that I am no longer under the curse of the law because Christ became a curse for me. I receive the free gift of life in Christ and choose to abide in Him. I renounce striving for perfection by living under the law. By Your grace, heavenly Father, I choose from this day forward to walk by faith in the power of Your Holy Spirit according to what You have said is true. In Jesus's name I pray. Amen.

Eating Disorders or Self-Mutilation

Dear heavenly Father, I renounce the lie that my value as a person is dependent upon my appearance or performance. I renounce cutting or abusing myself, vomiting, using laxatives or starving myself as a means of being in control, altering my appearance, or trying to cleanse myself of evil. I announce that only the blood of the Lord Jesus Christ cleanses me from sin. I realize that I have been bought with a price and that my body, which is the temple of the Holy Spirit, belongs to God. Therefore, I choose to glorify God in my body. I renounce the lie that I am evil or that any part of my body is evil. Thank You that You accept me just the way I am in Christ. In Jesus's name I pray. Amen.

Substance Abuse

Dear heavenly Father, I confess that I have misused substances (alcohol, tobacco, food, prescription or street drugs) for the purpose of pleasure, to escape reality, or to cope with difficult problems. I confess that I have abused my body and programmed my mind in harmful ways. I have quenched the Holy Spirit as well. Thank You for Your forgiveness. I renounce any satanic connection or influence in my life through my misuse of food or chemicals. I cast my anxieties onto Christ, who loves me. I commit myself to yielding no longer to substance abuse, but instead I choose to allow the Holy Spirit to direct and empower me. In Jesus's name I pray. Amen.

Gambling

Dear heavenly Father, I confess that I have been a poor steward of the financial resources that have been in my possession. I have gambled away my future chasing a false god. I have not been content with food and clothing, and the love of money has driven me to behave irrationally and sinfully. I renounce making provision for my flesh with regard to this lust. I commit myself to staying away from all gambling casinos, gambling websites, bookmakers, and lottery sales. I choose to believe that I am alive in Christ and dead to sin. Fill me with Your Holy Spirit so that I don't carry out the desires of the flesh. Show me the way of escape when I am tempted to return to my addictive behaviors. I stand against all of Satan's accusations, temptations, and deceptions by putting on the armor of God and standing firm in my faith. I choose to believe that You will meet all my needs according Your riches in glory. In Jesus's name I pray. Amen.

Bigotry

Dear heavenly Father, You have created all humanity in Your image. I confess that I have judged others by the color of their skin, their national origin, their social or economic status, their cultural differences, and their sexual orientation. I renounce racism, elitism, and sexism. I choose to believe "there is neither Jew nor Greek, there is neither slave nor free man, there is neither male nor female; for you are all one in Christ" (Galatians 3:28). Please show me the roots of my bigotry that I may confess them and be cleansed from such defilement. I pledge myself "to walk in a manner worthy of the calling with which [I] have been called, with all humility and gentleness, with patience, showing tolerance for one another in love, being diligent to preserve the unity of the Spirit in the bond of peace" (Ephesians 4:1-3). In Jesus's name I pray. Amen.

STEP 7

Curses Versus Blessings

The next step to freedom is to renounce the sins of your ancestors as well as any curses that may have been placed on you by deceived and evil people or groups.

Exodus 20:4-6 deals with the need for this step. How would you describe that need?

What conditions can contribute toward causing someone to struggle with a particular sin?

Ask the Lord to show you specifically what sins are characteristic of your family by praying the following prayer:

> *Dear heavenly Father, please reveal to my mind all the sins of my ancestors that have been passed down through family lines. As a new creation in Christ, I want to experience my freedom from those influences and to walk in my new identity as a child of God. In Jesus's name I pray. Amen.*

As the Lord brings those areas of family sin to your mind, list them on a separate sheet of paper.

In order to walk free from the sins of your ancestors and any curses and assignments targeted against you, read the following declaration and pray the following prayer out loud.

Declaration

I here and now reject and disown all the sins of my ancestors. As one who has been delivered from the domain of darkness and transferred into the kingdom of God's Son, I declare myself to be free from those harmful influences. I am no longer "in Adam." I am now alive "in Christ." Therefore, I am the recipient of the blessings of God upon my life as I choose to love and obey Him. As one who has been crucified and raised with Christ and who sits with Him in heavenly places, I renounce any and all satanic attacks and assignments directed against me and my ministry. Every curse placed on me was broken when Christ became a curse for me by dying on the cross (Galatians 3:13). I reject any and every way in which Satan may claim ownership of me. I belong to the Lord Jesus Christ, who purchased me with His own precious blood. I declare myself to be fully and eternally signed over and committed to the Lord Jesus Christ. Therefore, having submitted to God, I now by His authority resist the devil, and I command every spiritual enemy of the Lord Jesus Christ to leave my presence. In putting on the armor of God, I stand against Satan's temptations, accusations, and deceptions. From this day forward, I will seek to do only the will of my heavenly Father. (See Galatians 3:13.)

Prayer

Dear heavenly Father, I come to You as Your child, bought out of slavery to sin by the blood of the Lord Jesus Christ. You are the Lord of the universe and the Lord of my life. I submit my body to You as a living and holy sacrifice. May You be glorified through my life and body. I now ask You to fill me with Your Holy Spirit. I commit myself to the renewing of my mind in order that I may prove that Your will is good, acceptable, and perfect for me. I desire nothing more than to be like You. I pray, believe, and do all this in the wonderful name of Jesus, my Lord and Savior. Amen.

MAINTAINING YOUR FREEDOM

What things can you do to maintain the freedom you have gained?

Upon whom must you always depend for your freedom?

Freedom will be yours as long as you keep choosing the truth and standing firm in the strength of the Lord. Some people have found it helpful to walk through The Steps to Freedom in Christ when they feel the need to do so again. To maintain your freedom in Christ, I strongly suggest the following as well:

1. Get rid of or destroy any cult or occult objects in your home. (See Acts 19:18-20.)

2. Be part of a church where God's truth is taught with kindness and grace, and get involved in a small group where you can be honest and real.

3. Read and meditate on the truths of God's Word each day.

4. Don't let your mind be passive, especially concerning what you watch and listen to (Internet, music, TV, etc.). Actively take every thought captive to the obedience of Christ.

5. Be a good steward of your health and develop a godly lifestyle of rest, exercise, and proper diet.

6. Say the following daily prayer for the next 40 days, and the other prayers as needed.

Daily Prayer and Declaration

Dear heavenly Father, I praise You and honor You as my Lord and Savior. You are in control of all things. I thank You that

You are always with me and will never leave me nor forsake me. You are the only all-powerful and all-wise God. You are kind and loving in all Your ways. I love You and thank You that I am united with Jesus and spiritually alive in Him.

I choose not to love the world or the things in the world, and I crucify the flesh and all its passions. Thank You for the life I now have in Christ. I ask You to fill me with the Holy Spirit so I can be guided by You and not carry out the desires of the flesh. I declare my total dependence upon You and I take my stand against Satan and all his lying ways. I choose to believe the truths in Your Word despite what my feelings may say.

I refuse to be discouraged; You are the God of all hope. Nothing is too difficult for You. I am confident that You will supply all my needs as I seek to live according to Your Word. I thank You that I can be content and live a responsible life through Christ, who strengthens me.

I now take my stand against Satan and command him and all his evil spirits to depart from me. I choose to put on the full armor of God so I may be able to stand firm against all the devil's schemes. I submit my body as a living and holy sacrifice to You, and I choose to renew my mind by Your living Word. By so doing I will be able to prove that Your will is good, acceptable, and perfect for me. In the name of my Lord and Savior Jesus Christ I pray. Amen.

Bedtime Prayer

Thank You, Lord, that You have brought me into Your family and have blessed me with every spiritual blessing in the heavenly places in Christ Jesus. Thank You for this time of renewal and refreshment through sleep. I accept it as one of Your blessings for Your children, and I trust You to guard my mind and my body during my sleep. As I have thought about You and Your truth during the day, I choose to let those good thoughts continue in my mind while I am asleep. I commit myself to

You for Your protection against every attempt of Satan and his demons to attack me as I sleep. Guard my mind from nightmares. I renounce all fear and cast every anxiety upon You. I commit myself to You as my rock, my fortress, and my strong tower. May Your peace be upon this place of rest. In the strong name of the Lord Jesus Christ I pray. Amen.

Prayer for Spiritual Cleansing of Home/Apartment/Room

After removing and destroying all objects of false worship, pray this prayer out loud in every room:

Dear heavenly Father, I acknowledge that You are the Lord of heaven and earth. In Your sovereign power and love, You have entrusted many things to me. Thank You for this place where I live. I claim my home as a place of spiritual safety for me and my family, and I ask for Your protection from all the attacks of the enemy. As a child of God raised up and seated with Christ in the heavenly places, I command every evil spirit claiming ground in this place—based on the activities of past or present occupants, including me and my family—to leave and never return. I renounce all demonic assignments directed against this place. I ask You, heavenly Father, to post Your holy angels around this place to guard it from any and all attempts of the enemy to enter and disturb Your purposes for me and my family. I thank You, Father, for doing this in the name of the Lord Jesus Christ. Amen.

Prayer for Living in a Non-Christian Environment

After removing and destroying all objects of false worship in your home, pray this out loud in the place where you live:

Thank You, heavenly Father, for a place to live and to be renewed by sleep. I ask You to set aside my room [or portion of this room] as a place of spiritual safety for me. I renounce any allegiance given to false gods or spirits by other occupants. I renounce any claim to this room [space] by Satan based on the activities of past or present occupants, including me. On the basis of my position as a child of God and joint heir with Christ, who has all authority in heaven and on earth, I command all evil spirits to leave this place and never return. I ask You, heavenly Father, to station Your holy angels around me to protect me while I live here. In Jesus's mighty name I pray. Amen.

Continue to walk in the truth that your identity and sense of worth comes through who you are in Christ. Renew your mind with the truth that your *acceptance, security,* and *significance* are in Christ alone.

FREEDOM IN CHRIST MINISTRIES BOOKS AND RESOURCES

CORE MATERIAL

Victory Over the Darkness offers a study guide, audiobook, and DVD (Bethany House Publishers, 2000). With more than 1,400,000 copies in print, this core book explains who you are in Christ, how to walk by faith in the power of the Holy Spirit, how to be transformed by the renewing of your mind, how to experience emotional freedom, and how to relate to one another in Christ.

The Bondage Breaker offers a study guide and audiobook (Harvest House Publishers, 2018). This book explains spiritual warfare, what our protection is, ways that we are vulnerable, and how we can live a liberated life in Christ.

Discipleship Counseling (Bethany House Publishers, 2003) combines the concepts of discipleship and counseling and teaches the practical integration of theology and psychology for helping Christians resolve their personal and spiritual conflicts through repentance and faith in God.

The Steps to Freedom in Christ and accompanying interactive video (Bethany House Publishers, 2017) is a discipleship counseling tool that helps Christians resolve their personal and spiritual conflicts through genuine repentance and faith in God.

Restored (E3 Resources) is an expansion of The Steps to Freedom in Christ with additional explanations and instructions.

Walking in Freedom (Bethany House Publishers, 2008) is a 21-day devotional used for follow-up after leading someone through The Steps to Freedom.

Freedom in Christ (Bethany House Publishers, 2017) is a discipleship course for Sunday school classes and small groups. The course comes with a teacher's guide, a student guide, and a DVD covering 12 lessons and The Steps to Freedom in Christ. This course is designed to enable believers to resolve personal and spiritual conflicts and be established alive and free in Christ.

The Bondage Breaker DVD Experience (Harvest House Publishers, 2011) is also a discipleship course for Sunday school classes and small groups. It is similar to the one above, but the lessons are 15 minutes long instead of 30 minutes. It offers a student guide, but no teacher's guide.

"Victory Series" (Bethany House Publishers, 2014, 2015) is a comprehensive curriculum, including eight books that follow the growth sequence of being rooted in Christ, growing in Christ, living in Christ, and overcoming in Christ: *God's Story for You; Your New Identity; Your Foundation in Christ; Renewing Your Mind; Growing in Christ; Your Life in Christ; Your Authority in Christ; Your Ultimate Victory.*

The Bondage Breaker, The Next Step (Harvest House Publishers, 2011) has several testimonies of people who found their freedom from all kinds of problems, along with commentary by Dr. Anderson. It is an important learning tool for encouragers and gives hope to those who are entangled in sin.

Overcoming Addictive Behavior with Mike Quarles (Bethany House Publishers, 2003) explores the path to addiction and how a Christian can overcome addictive behaviors.

Overcoming Depression with Joanne Anderson (Bethany House Publishers, 2004) explores the nature of depression, which is a body, soul, and spirit problem. This resource presents a wholistic answer for overcoming this "common cold" of mental illnesses.

Daily in Christ with Joanne Anderson (Harvest House Publishers, 2000) is a popular daily devotional read by thousands of Internet subscribers every day.

Who I Am in Christ (Bethany House Publishers, 2001) has 36 short chapters describing who believers are in Christ and how their deepest needs are met in Him.

Freedom from Addiction with Mike and Julia Quarles (Bethany House Publishers, 1997) begins with Mike and Julia's journey into addiction and codependency, and explains the nature of chemical addictions and how to overcome them in Christ.

One Day at a Time with Mike Quarles (Bethany House Publishers, 2000) is a 365-day devotional that helps those who struggle with addictive behaviors and explains how to discover the grace of God on a daily basis.

Letting Go of Fear with Rich Miller (Harvest House Publishers, 2017) explains the nature of fear, anxiety, and panic attacks, and how to overcome them.

Setting Your Church Free with Charles Mylander (Bethany House Publishers, 2006, 2014) explains servant leadership and how the leaders of a church can resolve corporate conflicts through corporate repentance.

Setting Your Marriage Free with Charles Mylander (Bethany House Publishers, 2006, 2014) explains God's divine plan for marriage and the steps that couples can take to resolve their difficulties.

Christ-Centered Therapy with Dr. Terry and Julie Zuehlke (Zondervan Publishing House, 2000) explains the practical integration of theology and psychology for professional counselors and provides them with biblical tools for therapy.

Managing Anger with Rich Miller (Harvest House Publishers, 2018) explains the nature of anger and how to put away all anger, wrath, and malice.

Grace That Breaks the Chains with Rich Miller and Paul Travis (Harvest House Publishers, 2003, 2014) explains the bondage of legalism and how to overcome it by the grace of God.

Winning the Battle Within (Harvest House Publishers, 2008) shares God's standards for sexual conduct, examines the path to sexual addiction, and presents how to overcome sexual strongholds.

Restoring Broken Relationships (Bethany House Publishers, 2008) explains the primary ministry of the church, and how we can be reconciled to God and each other.

Rough Road to Freedom (Monarch Books) is Dr. Anderson's memoir.

The Power of Presence (Monarch Books) is about experiencing the presence of God during difficult times and what our presence means to each other. This book is written in the context of Dr. Anderson caring for his wife, who recently died from agitated dementia.

To learn more about Harvest House books and
to read sample chapters, visit our website:

www.harvesthousepublishers.com

HARVEST HOUSE PUBLISHERS
EUGENE, OREGON